Book, Music, & Lyrics by

JACOB RICHMOND & BROOKE MAXWELL

ISBN 978-0-8222-4592-6

www.concordtheatricals.com
www.concordtheatricals.co.uk

FOR PRODUCTION INQUIRIES

UNITED STATES AND CANADA
info@concordtheatricals.com
1-866-979-0447

UNITED KINGDOM AND EUROPE
licensing@concordtheatricals.co.uk
020-7054-7298

Each title is subject to availability from Concord Theatricals Corp., depending upon country of performance. Please be aware that *RIDE THE CYCLONE* may not be licensed by Concord Theatricals Corp. in your territory. Professional and amateur producers should contact the nearest Concord Theatricals Corp. office or licensing partner to verify availability.

This work is published by Samuel French, an imprint of Concord Theatricals Corp.

MUSIC AND THIRD-PARTY MATERIALS USE NOTE

IMPORTANT BILLING AND CREDIT REQUIREMENTS

CHARACTERS

The Choir

OCEAN O'CONNELL ROSENBERG, 17, belter, alto/soprano

MISCHA BACHINSK, 18, rapper/folk singer, baritone

NOEL GRUBER, 17, smooth cabaret voice, tenor

RICKY POTTS, 17, rock voice, baritone

CONSTANCE BLACKWOOD, 17, rock voice, alto

JANE DOE, ?, classical/operatic voice, soprano

Narrator

THE AMAZING KARNAK, a mechanical fortune-telling machine. A deep, rumbling baritone voice, with a steady, measured, calm inflection that exudes gravitas, but it is never pushed to comedic extremes. There is no archness in the voice. Think an ominous mechanical Santa Claus—or God—or Hal 3000.

The Band: Virgil and the Underworlds

VIRGIL THE RAT, bass player, ideally should be able to play upright and electric. Although a rare bird, ideally Virgil can also play the cello.

Assuming Virgil can play the cello, the quintet is comprised of a group of rats. The band consists of a pianist/accordionist, a keyboard 2 player filling in the blanks, a guitarist (acoustic, electric) and a percussionist/drummer (who can play glockenspiel when asked). Ideally, the band can also chorally support the choir.

Prerecorded backtracks (BT) may support the band in the electronic sections of the piece—or in sections that require a larger sound. (For example, the heavily processed sounds of "This Song Is Awesome" sound best with a programmed beat.)

SETTING

A dilapidated warehouse; stored in it, the debris of a once-thriving amusement park. There is the detritus of many rides, midway booths, marquees…their once-brilliant colors now muted with age and neglect.

Over all of this colorful rust is a massive broken iron girder of the Cyclone roller coaster; it stands in massive relief to the scale of the other rides at the fairground. This colossal, curved girder alludes to a horrible accident with the grotesque nature in which the iron bends at a specific place in its curvature—it too is covered in rust—yet upon the girder, a thick patch of vines has grown at its base… The vines intertwine in the curvature, almost growing throughout the girder. To the right of the girder is a massive marquee for the ride that reads "CYCLONE," hung from several chains… One of the support chains has been eaten through with rust entirely, making the marquee hang oddly—sadly.

At the center of the stage is a miniature proscenium with a lush red scallop curtain that opens to the sides. Its once-grand moldings are cracked and the plaster chipped away…

Above the miniature proscenium is a withered round billboard that once stood above the entry gate for the fair. It reads "WONDERVILLE! World Class Fun at Prairie Prices!" and has the image of a looping roller coaster on it. This sign shall serve as the main projection screen for projection sequences unless otherwise specified.

To the side of the proscenium is a carnie prize booth with a light-up marquee that reads "Prizes"… This is where the band lives. The booth should have a scrim in front of it so that it is possible to hide the band when unlit.

The warehouse itself looks as if it was packed hastily and that Nature has begun to reclaim it. Mold, vines, even breaks of dirt through the concrete of the warehouse floor have begun to grow patches of fungus and little triumphant patches of grass.

TIME

The action in the musical takes place a year behind the present, narrated by the Amazing Karnak, who exists in the very distant future. The idea being that he is telling a story a couple decades after "The Accident."

AUTHORS' NOTES

Casting

The authors give full license to any performer playing any role in the musical. While pronoun changes are fine to accommodate performers' interpretation, any changes to the book or lyrics beyond these changes must be cleared by the authors and Concord Theatricals. (For instance, Karnak has been changed to Cassandra to accommodate a female performer in the past.)

Costumes

All the kids wear Saint Cassian uniforms, the colors being gray and blue. Boys wear gray dress pants, white dress shirts, ties, and blue vests. Girls wear gray tunics, white shirts, and ties. The way they wear their uniforms is character dependent.

Sound Design

Gritty midway carnival sounds should be used throughout...old school and lo-fi, but ideally NOT modern, slick, or digital.

Sound Effects

An optional sound effects package is available for purchase through Concord Theatricals; cues for the package are listed throughout the script. A few key notes on these sound effects:

- "Photobomb" effects are intended to be paired with the onstage action of the Karnak lever pull.
- Prerecorded "Bumper" tracks are included in the package for your reference and usage, if you choose not to have a live band play them.
- "SFX #19A.2 Low B Flat Buzz" is designed to give the opening pitch for "Music #20. Sailing Reprise." This can also be covered by the live band or other tracks, depending on the needs of your production.
- All tracks are, of course, to be used at your discretion. Feel free to utilize your own sound effects in place of any provided.

Playing Style

Although it's tempting to play the work in a large, cartoonish fashion, this will not line up with the playing style required to make the second half of the musical resonate. Although the characters are larger-than-life in parts, it is urged that they are grounded in real intentions and motivations throughout the piece.

Projections

Not simply an enhancement to the narrative, these sequences are pivotal in the narrative of this show.

RIDE THE CYCLONE

[MUSIC #1: Dream of Life Opening]

We barely see a figure with its back to the audience in a Saint Cassian girl's tunic, as if she is lit by the faintest beam of moonlight. Although we see her body, her head seems to be entirely missing in her silhouette.

JANE.
I KNOW THIS DREAM OF LIFE IS NEVER-ENDING
IT GOES AROUND AND ROUND AND ROUND AGAIN
YOU KNOW THE SUN IS RISING WHILE DESCENDING
IT GOES ON AND ON AND NEVER ENDS

At the end, Jane Doe magically disappears. In darkness…

[MUSIC #1A: Amazing Karnak Organ]

A mechanical fortune-telling machine is revealed, à la 1920s penny arcade. The fortune teller is an imposing figure with a majestic beard and glowing eyes.

KARNAK. Hello. I am the Amazing Karnak. This is not a boast but rather what it says on my legal patent as a precognition machine. I was designed to predict the exact cause, time, and place of someone's death. A rather morbid function, I grant you, which is precisely why I was set on "family-fun novelty mode" when sold to the Wonderville traveling fairground… Turns out…being told the place and time of your death in front of your family, with a mouthful of corn dog at a fairground, is the very opposite of fun. I can even predict my own demise. I always could—tonight in this warehouse, in a little over an hour.

[MUSIC #1B: Virgil Bass Solo]

We see a projection of a rat running across the projection screen through the following text.

Meet my executioner, a rat I've named Virgil. For the last two years, Virgil has steadily been chewing on my power cable. In a little over an hour, Virgil shall chew his way through the rubber, biting down on two hundred volts of electricity...instantly killing us both. As there is nothing more base than Death...I've decided for tonight's concert, Virgil shall play the bass.

We see the life-sized version of Virgil, a human-sized rat, who appears to do a very skilled, short bass solo.

[MUSIC #2: Karnak Organ Pt. 2/Uranium]

Before we begin, let me lay down some ground rules. The first rule: One that has baffled theatregoers since the days of Aeschylus...the armrest to your left is yours, the one to your right is your neighbor's. If you believe that both armrests are yours exclusively...you are part of the problem. Also, please turn off your cell phones. I assure you that none of the calls you are about to receive will have life-altering consequences...except for one of you...my most sincere condolences. Accidents happen.

The curtains part and the choir appears.

Speaking of which, ladies and gentlemen, I give you the Saint Cassian Chamber Choir of Uranium City, Saskatchewan:

The choir, hunched over almost lifeless... As they enter the stage, they seem to be resurrecting before our eyes. Once they are in place, a swoosh [SFX #2.1: Resurrection Swoosh] as they jerk back to life, ending with them snapping up into their choir formation. The piano vamp on "Uranium" starts immediately.

OCEAN. I thank you, dear adjudicator, for considering the Saint Cassian Chamber Choir for our senior concert.

KARNAK. This is them on Monday, September 14th.

OCEAN. We are thrilled to be here, yet again, at the Kiwanis International singing competition. Last year we came in second place.

KARNAK. They were the only choir in competition.

OCEAN. This just shows the high standards of excellence in Kiwanis—even in competition against yourself, you can still walk away a loser. Constance?

CONSTANCE. *(Reading.)* "Our first song is by Father Louis P. Marcus, our choir conductor... He was inspired by traditional African folk music—specifically *The Lion King*."

Constance gives a "That can't be right" expression. Ocean prompts her to continue.

It's about our hometown, Uranium. Enjoy.

Throughout the first part of this movement, Ricky Potts plays the tambourine and visibly hates every minute of it. Mischa is barely paying attention, stealing moments to look at his phone, to the irritation of Ocean. The choreography for this first section is that of a small-town choir; imagine that it has been choreographed by an eighty-six-year-old Catholic priest.

OCEAN.
URANIUM

KIDS (EXCEPT RICKY).
URANIUM
THAT'S OUR TOWN, OUR FRIENDLY
TOWN

OCEAN.
URANIUM

KIDS (EXCEPT RICKY).
URANIUM
THAT'S OUR TOWN, OUR HIGHWAY
TOWN

NOEL.
THE SKY IS ALMOST BLUE HERE
GRAIN ELEVATORS TOO HERE

KIDS (EXCEPT RICKY and NOEL).
OOO

KIDS (EXCEPT RICKY).
THE PRIDE AND JOY OF SWEET
SASKATCHEWAN

CONSTANCE.
WE CAME HERE
FOR THE HALF-LIFE
AND STAYED HERE
FOR OUR WHOLE LIFE

KIDS (EXCEPT RICKY and CONSTANCE).
OOO

KIDS (EXCEPT RICKY).
TO GIVE THE WHOLE WIDE WORLD PLUTONIUM

OCEAN.
URANIUM

KIDS (EXCEPT RICKY).
URANIUM
THAT'S OUR TOWN, OUR FRIENDLY TOWN
OH NO NO
WE WILL NEVER LEAVE THIS TOWN AT ALL

The lights shifts starkly, and the children float around the space in bewildered unease.

[MUSIC #3: Minor Turn]

KARNAK.
Tonight I shall speak of these teenagers, whose tales ended abruptly on a roller coaster in a small Canadian town in the middle of nowhere. The Saint Cassian Chamber Choir.
And my part in this story…
I read all of the children's fortunes
I felt their hopes,
thoughts, dreams,

…knowing they would board the doomed roller coaster and could tell them nothing. I even suggested that they ride the Cyclone. On Monday, September 14th, they would board the Cyclone roller coaster at 6:17 p.m. At 6:19 p.m, this same roller coaster's front axle would break, causing it to derail at the apex of the loop-de-loop, hurtling the children to their deaths.

KIDS (EXCEPT JANE).
LA LA LA LA LA
LA LA LA LA LA LA LA LA LA
LA LA LA LA LA
LA LA LA LA LA LA LA LA LA

LA LA LA LA LA LA LA LA
LA LA LA LA LA LA LA LA
LA LA LA LA LA LA LA LA
LA LA LA LA LA LA LA LA

KIDS.
AH
(AH)
AH
(AH)
LA LA LA LA LA LA LA LA
LA
AH
(AH)
AH
(AH)
AH

KIDS (EXCEPT RICKY).
AND THEN YOU'RE SAILING THROUGH SPACE
YOU DON'T KNOW UP FROM DOWN
AND YOU FEEL A LITTLE STRANGE
FROM ALL THAT SPINNING ROUND

AND EVERYTHING YOU LOVED
AND EVERYTHING YOU DREAMED
AND EVERYTHING YOU FEARED
AND EVERYTHING THAT SEEMED SO
OH SO TERRIFYING

Band echo.

IT'S FAR BEHIND, ON THE GROUND
LIKE OUR FAR FROM THE CITY

LITTLE ITTY-BITTY PRETTY HOMETOWN
JUST A TEENY TINY DOT, ON A WEE BLUE BALL
AND WE'VE ALL BEEN SPINNING…

BOYS.
ALL BEEN SPINNING

KIDS.
ROUND 'N ROUND 'N
ROUND
'N ROUND 'N ROUND
ROUND 'N ROUND, 'N
ROUND 'N ROUND 'N
ROUND
'N ROUND 'N ROUND,
HOO!

BOYS.	**GIRLS.**
URA—	EMPTY STREETS OF EMPTY SHOPS
NIUM	SHUTTERED ROWS OF MOM-AND-POPS
URA—	BOW DOWN TO THE MEGA
NIUM	SHOPPING MALL
SMART ONES ALL	URA—
PACKED UP AND WENT	
WHY STAY IF YOU CAN'T	NIUM
PAY THE RENT	
WE WILL NEVER	URA—
LEAVE THIS TOWN	
AT ALL	NIUM

KIDS.
DRINK SOME BREW, JOIN THE CHOIR
BUILD YOURSELF A FUNERAL PYRE
URANIUM OUR DEAD-END DIVE
WE'LL NEVER LEAVE THIS TOWN ALIVE
NO, WE WILL NEVER LEAVE THIS TOWN AT ALL!

KARNAK. *(Spoken in rhythm.)* Greetings children, it's time to play!

KIDS.
EARTH IS SKY AND SKY IS GROUND
(Whispered.) DID WE FINALLY LEAVE OUR TOWN?

The children stand, gobsmacked, huddled together.

OCEAN. Where are we?

[SFX #3.1: Karnak start up]

MECHANICAL VOICE. You have inserted t-t-t-t-two…loonies! KARNAK! He sees the future!

OCEAN. *(To Karnak.)* Look, what is this, what is happening?!

KARNAK. Meet Ocean O'Connell Rosenberg.

[SFX #3.2: Meet Ocean]

Catchphrase:

Ocean in a light special, forms an Ocean pose.

OCEAN. Democracy rocks!

[SFX #3.3: Wind sound, light restore (Ocean)]

Lights restore.

What the heck was that?

KARNAK. Your catchphrase. In the interest of the expedition of time, I've taken the liberty of choreographing a few of your moves in advance. Don't bore us; get to the chorus. Our time together is limited.

OCEAN. You said "play" earlier. What exactly are we playing? Is this a game?

[SFX #3.4: Select game mode]

KARNAK. Ocean has selected *game mode*!!

Group grumbles.

OCEAN. What? *(To choir.)* Guys, I really didn't… *(Directly.)* What game?

*A prize wall is exposed with crushed cigarettes, a Hello Kitty cupcake, and an Iron Maiden T-shirt.**

KARNAK. A game with fabulous prizes: Like a stale pack of menthol Kools.

[SFX #3.5: Prize 1—Menthol Kools]

A deep-fried Hello Kitty cupcake!!

[SFX #3.6: Prize 2—Cupcake]

This limited-edition Iron Maiden T-shirt still ripe with the pong of the carnie that wore it.

[SFX #3.7: Prize 3—T-Shirt]

OCEAN. Look, what is going *on*?!

KARNAK. Perhaps you might be interested in the grand prize, Ocean?

One worthy contestant will be brought back to life…

[SFX #3.8: The grand prize]

…to live beyond the Cyclone accident.

Behind the curtain, a blinding white light, and a tunnel of smoke… a howling wind can be heard…

[MUSIC #4: The Other Side]

KIDS.
SOMEWHERE SUNRISE BEGINS ANOTHER DAY
BEGINS ANOTHER DAY

The curtain drops.

KARNAK. The grand prize—to live again.

CONSTANCE. That's way better than a Hello Kitty cupcake.

KARNAK. Meet Constance Blackwood.

[SFX #4.1: Meet Constance]

Catchphrase:

Constance in a light special.

CONSTANCE. Sorry…

[SFX #4.2: Wind sound, light restore (Constance)]

Lights restore.

The following interchange moves at an incredible speed.

OCEAN. Why only one of us, why not all of us?

KARNAK. Sadly, I've only ever possessed the power to bring one back to life.

OCEAN. What do we have to do to be brought back to life?

KARNAK. "The one who wants to win it the most shall redeem the loser—in order to complete the whole."

OCEAN. That doesn't make any sense.

KARNAK. I trade mostly in prophecies that don't make any sense—until they actually do.

OCEAN. I take it you are the judge?

[SFX #4.3: Sad bassoon]

KARNAK. It appears Ocean O'Connell Rosenberg has used up the group's three questions for this evening.

All except Ocean and Constance audibly grunt, but not cartoonishly.

NOEL. *(Under his breath.)* Even in death I can't escape her. She followed me to the afterlife. Well played, Satan, well played.

KARNAK. Meet Noel Gruber:

[SFX #4.4: Meet Noel]

Aspiring poet laureate. Catchphrase?

Noel in a light special.

[MUSIC #4A: Noel's Catchphrase Underscore]

NOEL. Being the only gay man in a small rural high school is kind of like having a laptop in the Stone Age. I mean sure you can have one, but there's nowhere to plug it in.

[SFX #4A.1: Wind sound, light restore (Noel)]

Lights restore.

OCEAN. But that's not fair, you didn't tell me there were only three questions.

KARNAK. I believe I did. After the fact.

MISCHA. *(To himself, under his breath, sounding like DMX.)* Yo! I can't get no Wi-Fi up in this bitch.

KARNAK. Meet Mischa Bachinski—

[SFX #4A.2: Meet Mischa]

Ukrainian bad boy. Catchphrase:

[MUSIC #4B: Mischa's Catchphrase Underscore]

Mischa in a light special.

MISCHA. My gangsta persona is just armor to conceal that I am a naked child wandering through the wilderness, holding in my hands my wounded, fragile heart.

Mischa does a delicate pirouette.

[SFX #4B.1: Wind sound, light restore (Mischa)]

Lights restore.

He snaps out of it, recovering.

(To himself, humiliated.) That was emasculating.

RICKY. Story of my life, brother.

Kids gasp.

CONSTANCE. Oh my god, Ricky! You can talk!

RICKY. That's nothing…watch this…

Ricky does literally any virtuosic party trick that the performer can offer: magic, juggling, the splits, guitar shred, anything…to show that Ricky immediately knows that this world has no boundaries.

KARNAK. Meet Richard Potts—

[SFX #4B.2: Meet Ricky]

Town dreamer. Catchphrase:

[MUSIC #4C: Ricky's Catchphrase Underscore]

Ricky in a light special.

RICKY. *(Reverb, big sound like a video game.)* Level up!

[SFX #4C.1: Wind sound, light restore (Ricky)]

Lights restore. Ricky snaps out of it.

OCEAN. This couldn't possibly get any weirder…

KARNAK. I'm under the firm belief that it always can… Allow me to introduce you to the mystery contestant…

[MUSIC #5: Jane Doe's Entrance]

The curtain slowly rises, spilling with smoke. Jane Doe is revealed. A haunting figure with blonde dolly locks, white face, and black eyes. She clutches a headless doll… Jane moves like a marionette with broken strings. For haunting effect, her mic has reverb on it, which continues throughout the entire show.

KIDS.
OO
OO
AH
AH

JANE.	**KIDS (EXCEPT JANE).**
(Sing-talking, childlike.) Jane Doe is what the coroner said,	OO
They found my body, not my head	
No parents came, and so they never learned	OO
my name, or who I used to be.	AH
My life, an unsolved mystery.	AH
From ashes I was made, and ashes I return.	OO
And so I walk alone and wonder why…	OO

WHY? AH
WHY? AH
WHY? AH

Lights restore. The kids stare at her, slack-jawed. Jane stares, fixed on Constance.

CONSTANCE. Did anybody just pee themselves a little?

Beat.

Me neither.

JANE. *(To Constance.)* Do you want to brush my dolly's hair?

CONSTANCE. *(To Ocean.)* I'm really freaked out right now!

JANE. Do you want to know what really freaks me out?

CONSTANCE. Mmmm...not-really-ever-at-all-really-sorry.

KARNAK. Meet Jane Doe. Catchphrase:

Lights suddenly down only on Jane.

[MUSIC #5A: Jane's Catchphrase Underscore]

JANE. *(In one breath.)* When a lioness has children, she stops making love to the lion. The lion gets jealous, sometimes so jealous he eats the children. You'd think this would upset the lioness. Far from it, they make love again, like the children never existed. I find that idea terrifying.

Beat.

CONSTANCE. I'm going to stand a little farther away from you, okay?

[MUSIC #5B: Snare Roll]

Lights circle around the theatre. Constance runs over to Ocean; Jane follows her. Ocean runs over to Karnak; Constance follows Ocean. At the end of the snare, the follow spot lands on Ocean.

KARNAK. Ocean Rosenberg...you are first.

OCEAN. Why?

KARNAK. Alas, if only you hadn't burned off those three questions right at the top.

OCEAN. It's just, when you tie the room together...I think Constance is going to seem like the natural choice for that slot.

CONSTANCE. You want me to go first?

OCEAN. Oh, if you insist, um...Mister Whatever? I think Constance and I are going to tradesies.

KARNAK. *(Flatly.)* No tradesies.

OCEAN. *(Without skipping a beat.)* Well I'm happy about that actually. Sure, I'll go first. I just want to say two things… First, I don't know how it is in your culture, but in ours, playing games where people's lives are on the table? Super illegal. Second, so inspiring. That a man encased in a literal box, has learned to think outside of it.

Claps.

[MUSIC #6: Ocean's Bumper]

The first bumper—Ocean's. The bumpers are moments when the specified character approaches Karnak to have their fortune read while he narrates, underscored by thematic music relevant to the character. The rest of the characters rearrange the scene and also participate in a visual retelling of the mini-biography.

KARNAK. Ocean O'Connell Rosenberg, born December 22nd, Capricorn: the ambitious nature.

[SFX #6.1: Ocean's photobomb]

Ocean pulls Karnak's lever. The first photomontage occurs, with SFX—a flurry of portraits of Ocean from babyhood to seventeen.

Favorite ride: the bumper cars.

Ocean does a bumper car gesture.

Ocean was born into a family of far-left-of-center humanists who moved to Northern Saskatchewan to live a carbon-free lifestyle.

Jane and Mischa enter as Ocean's parents, hippy dancing. Jane is still lost. No matter what character she is playing, she does the role stiffly.

The hemp needlepoint sign above the household's toilet read: "If it's yellow, let it mellow. If it's brown…scoop it out with your hand and put it in the compost." Yet in between all the drum circles, Marxist parables, and cheese sandwiches made of human breast milk…Ocean could never shake the feeling she was the white sheep of her family. It was only at the age of eight, when she found amongst her parents' record collection an album called *Up with People…*

Constance, Noel, and Ricky enter with matching ties and collars as in Up with People…super chirpy.

The cloying positivity of this procapitalist gaggle of teen crooners brought tears to her eyes. Perhaps the peppiest thing Halliburton has ever produced. High school president, straight-A student, Ocean O'Connell Rosenberg… the most successful girl in town.

Music out.

OCEAN. Judges, student body, colleagues, friends…ominous novelty machine…I had a speech prepared for this very occasion, but I simply cannot read it.

She rips a piece of paper.

MISCHA. *(To Noel.)* How could she have a speech for *this*?

OCEAN. I am just going to speak from my heart. I've known most of these folks since pre-K…I love them all…Constance Blackwood, my best friend forever, my BFF—

Constance is sitting next to Jane, who has locked eyes with her, giving her the thousand-mile stare.

CONSTANCE. Ocean, she's—

OCEAN. Don't interrupt, sweetie. Constance is the salt of the earth… Our "Mary Main Street" looking for her "Joe Six-Pack." Sure, she has some serious self-esteem issues, why wouldn't she? That's why I formed an improv duo, as a confidence-building exercise—sound off!

CONSTANCE and OCEAN. *(Performing a prerehearsed physical routine.)* Unlock the Power of the Positive! U-POP!

CONSTANCE. We get pretty crazy sometimes…

OCEAN. Constance Eleanor Blackwood. You know I find the word "crazy" offensive.

CONSTANCE. *(Gritting teeth.)* That's why Ocean scripts all our improvs in advance.

OCEAN. My time, Constance, my time…

She sits Constance back next to Jane, who locks eyes with her again while Constance grimaces.

Look, I've seen enough reality TV to get what you want us to do here… Who's the best? I mean sure, grades, humanitarian efforts, extracurricular activities, prestigious university, spiritual mastery of both Judaism and Catholicism. (Nailed my confirmation and bat mitzvah, in the same week!) And I'm not even bragging about that because it's against my Buddhist beliefs… I am the best here, by any metric of society, I get that…

Trembling voice breaking with emotion, she is moved by herself being moving.

…but if that's how worth is measured, I want no part of it! Look…some of us are left wing, some of us are right wing…but the last time I checked it takes two wings to fly!! We are community! We are Family! We are the World!

Constance claps enthusiastically; the other kids grudgingly clap—almost a Pavlovian response to Ocean's many speeches in their high school.

[SFX #6.2: Sad bassoon (Ocean concedes)]

KARNAK. Ocean O'Connell Rosenberg heroically concedes.

OCEAN. *(Ice.)* She does what?!

KARNAK. I respect you taking the moral high ground. Next.

[MUSIC #7: What the World Needs]

OCEAN. I'm just trying to prove to you that I'm a good person!

KARNAK. Duly noted. Next.

OCEAN. NO! NO! I'm urging you to make the responsible choice here. For the betterment of humanity.

WHAT THE WORLD NEEDS IS PEOPLE LIKE ME
TO KEEP IT ALL SPINNING AROUND

KIDS.

I'M THE MOVER, I'M THE SHAKER
I'M THE HEADLINE MAKER

OCEAN.

MM MM, I GET UP
OO OO OO, I GET UP
AND NO ONE'S GONNA KEEP ME DOWN

A general smarmy rap, seemingly to no one in particular, but obviously referring to the individual kids.

OKAY… IT'S CLEAR, I'M THE TOP OF THIS CLASS
THESE FOLKS HERE, WELL THEY PUMP THE GAS
FETCH ME A COFFEE, SHINE MY SHOES
SOME OF US ARE WINNERS, SOME WERE BORN TO LOSE

YOU GOT THE SANDWICH ARTIST, THE SECURITY GUARD?
THE WALMART GREETER WITH AN OVERDRAWN CREDIT CARD
HE "SMOKES GANJA," OOO, IT'S SO GROOVY
TO STAY AT HOME AND WATCH A TRANSFORMER MOVIE

SHE SERVES ME COKE AND A MEDIUM FRIES
AND NO THANKS, I DON'T WANT IT SUPERSIZED
'CAUSE THAT'S LOW-CLASS, DIABETES IN A CUP!
KEEP YOUR HEAD DOWN AND THINGS WILL LOOK UP

KIDS.

WHAT THE WORLD NEEDS IS PEOPLE LIKE ME
TO KEEP IT ALL SPINNING AROUND
I'M THE MOVER, I'M THE SHAKER
I'M THE HEADLINE MAKER

OCEAN.

MM MM, I GET UP

CONSTANCE.

SHE GETS UP

OCEAN.

I GET UP!
NO ONE'S GONNA KEEP ME DOWN!

(To Mischa in particular.) SERIOUSLY?
THIS ONE HERE? HE'S RARIN' TO FAIL?!
HE'LL ROB A 7-ELEVEN, AND GO STRAIGHT TO JAIL
MAYBE STEAL HUBCAPS, MAYBE STEAL BOOZE?
EXPRESSING HIMSELF WITH HIS HOMEMADE TATTOOS!

(To Constance.) SOCCER MOM, MINIVAN
FOUR LITTLE BRATS, NO STEADY MAN
DO WE REALLY NEED ANOTHER ORGAN DONOR?

Maybe that was a little harsh? Love you!

(To Ricky in particular.) AH NOO, COMIC BOOKS? *SPIDERMAN*?
THIS KID DOESN'T HAVE AN ATTENTION SPAN
NEVER REALLY HEARD FROM, ONLY EVER SEEN
(Whispered aside.) WE'RE BRINGIN' BACK THE DUDE
WHO PLAYS THE TAMBOURINE?!

KIDS.

WHAT THE WORLD NEEDS IS PEOPLE LIKE ME
TO KEEP IT ALL SPINNING AROUND
I'M THE MOVER, I'M THE SHAKER
I'M THE HEADLINE MAKER!

OCEAN.

I GET UP
MM MM MM

KIDS (EXCEPT OCEAN).

SHE GETS UP!

OCEAN.

I GET UP!
AND NO ONE'S GONNA

KEEP ME DOWN
AND AS WE

MOVE THROUGH LIFE
TO FIND OUR PLACE
IN THE CROWD

OO

SOME DON'T MAKE THE
CUT
THAT'S CRYSTAL
CLEAR-O

OH YES
OH YES, OH ISN'T
SOMEONE KEEPING SCORE?!
I'VE GOT TO SAY IT SO LOUD?!
I MEAN

KIDS.
DO WE REALLY NEED ANOTHER ZERO?
OR ZERO?
OR ZERO?
OR ZERO?
OR ZERO?

OCEAN.
ADD 'EM ALL UP, AND YOU
STILL GET ZERO!
WHAT YOU REALLY NEED IS
A MOTHER-LOVIN' HE—
—RO!

KIDS (EXCEPT OCEAN).
AND
OH OH

OCEAN.
HE'LL NEVER LEARN TO READ!

KIDS (EXCEPT OCEAN).
AND OH OH

OCEAN.
HE'S NEVER GONNA BREED!

KIDS (EXCEPT OCEAN).
AND OH OH

OCEAN.
GOING TO JAIL GUARANTEED!

KIDS (EXCEPT JANE).
AND SHE'S A FREAKY MONSTER!

KIDS (EXCEPT OCEAN).

YES, THERE'S A PROBLEM

OCEAN.

I'M THE SOLUTION
DARWIN HAD A THEORY CALLED…

She patronizingly coaxes the choir along.

KIDS (EXCEPT OCEAN).

EVOLUTION?

OCEAN.

HE PUT IT INTO
WORDS, BUT IT'S
PLAIN TO SEE
WE NEED A LITTLE
LESS OF THEM,
A LITTLE MORE
OF ME!

RICKY and MISCHA.	**JANE, CONSTANCE, and NOEL.**	**OCEAN.**
WHAT THE WORLD NEEDS	WE CAN'T ALL	ME
IS PEOPLE LIKE ME	BE HEROES	ME ME
TO KEEP IT ALL SPINNING	NO! MOST OF	ME ME,
AROUND	US?	ME ME
I'M THE	ZEROS	ME ME
MOVER, I'M THE SHAKER	SOME FLY	OH, OH,
I'M THE HEADLINE		OH, ME,
MAKER	HIGH	ME
MM, MM		
SHE GETS UP!		
	SHE GETS UP!	
SHE GETS UP		
OH WHAT THE		
WORLD NEEDS IS	WE CAN'T ALL	A LITTLE
PEOPLE LIKE ME	BE HEROES	BIT
TO KEEP IT ALL SPINNING	NO! MOST OF	MORE
AROUND	US?	OF ME
I'M THE	ZEROS	
MOVER, I'M THE SHAKER	SOME FLY	
I'M THE HEADLINE	HIGH	
MAKER		
MM, MM		
SHE GETS UP!		I GET UP!

SHE GETS UP!

SHE GETS UP!

I GET UP!

KIDS (EXCEPT OCEAN).
SOME STAY DOWN

OCEAN.
OCEAN'S GONNA TAKE YOU
DOWN
DOWN!

Ocean, who's still in her button pose—atop a human pyramid of her classmates—looks down.

OCEAN. *(Viciously/competitively.)* What a rush! Who's next?

KARNAK. Perhaps now would be a good time to say that whoever is brought back to life, will be brought back by a unanimous vote from each and every member of the choir.

Ocean's face goes white.

OCEAN. What?

KARNAK. Whoever comes back needs a unanimous vote from the choir.

OCEAN. But if I would have known that—

KARNAK. You wouldn't have called every one of your potential judges a loser, crowing about your superiority in song, culminating in you standing on top of them in a human pyramid? That did strike me as an unorthodox strategy.

Kids break out of the human pyramid, glaring at Ocean.

OCEAN. *(To Noel.)* What?

NOEL. What?! You just told your "best friend" that her greatest achievement in life will be to become an organ donor.

CONSTANCE. *(Head tilted, hearing the insult for the first time.)* I'm usually more of a melody person, less of a lyric person truthfully… "Organ donor"? Is that what you said?

OCEAN. I was in the moment…sorry Constance, I didn't mean—

CONSTANCE. Aw, it's okay…it kinda really super hurts but—

[MUSIC #7A: Jane Super Hurts]

JANE. Do you want to know what I find kind of really super hurts?

Constance politely slinks away from Jane's touch.

CONSTANCE. Maybe later, thanks. Sorry.

OCEAN. What I did there is exactly what you shouldn't do in this competition. You guys know I love you! *(To Mischa.)* Mischa, I love *you*! I even pretended to believe in your imaginary fiancée!

MISCHA. She is not my imaginary fiancée, she is my real fiancée—on my telephone.

OCEAN. I even celebrate your culturally-ingrained alcoholism. I mean the only reason you're in the choir is because you stole three boxes of communion wine.

MISCHA. It was my cousin's birthday... *(Proudly.)* In my country it is sacred tradition to take drink on birthday!

OCEAN. Your cousin was in grade four. He had to get his stomach pumped. *(Searchingly, to Noel.)* Noel, I love you! You challenged my preconceived notion that all gay dudes are fun to be around...

Noel looks directly at the audience, shaking his head, bemused.

(Desperately, to Ricky.) Ricky, I love you, Lil' Sweetie!

RICKY. Don't call me Lil' Sweetie.

OCEAN. I got you into the choir...even though you couldn't *talk*. I mean, you got to play the tambourine.

RICKY. No one *gets* to play the tambourine. They're always *made* to. No one's going home with the tambourine guy.

OCEAN. *(To Jane.)* And her...? *(Dripping with contempt.)* ...So even that thing gets a vote tonight, huh? *(Quickly shifting to positivity.)* But I love her! My song was a cautionary tale of hubris—you guys know I love you! *(Angry.)* I LOVE YOU! I LOVE YOU! I freakin' love YOU OKAY! So for my *real* number I'm going to sing about how much I love you guys...this song is simply called, "I Love You Guys."

[MUSIC #8: I Love You Guys]

I LOVE YOU GUYS...

The follow spot swings over to Noel.

NOEL. *(To the heavens.)* URGH! Sweet Jesus Christ on a bike, make her stop!

[MUSIC #9: Noel's Bumper]

KARNAK. Noel Gruber, born March 5th, Pisces: sign of passion.

[SFX #9.1: Noel's photobomb]

He pulls Karnak's side lever. A linear photomontage of baby pictures, child pictures, young teen pictures, ending with his current yearbook photo.

Favorite ride: the Ferris wheel. Very early on in Noel's life...his mother realized two things.

Beat.

The second was his penchant for all things nihilistic.

Ricky enters with a wand, zapping imaginary wizards.

While other children acted out *Harry Potter*, Noel acted out French New Wave cinema.

Noel grabs Ricky's wand, breaks it, and takes a drag from it, using it as a cigarette. Music fades into [SFX #9.2: Noel's wind].

In grade seven…during the Saint Cassian Christmas Nativity pageant, Noel was suspended for suddenly breaking into this excerpt from *Waiting for Godot.*

The scene below happens over sung underscoring.

ENSEMBLE.
LU LU LU LU
LU LU LU LU
LU LU LU LU

Noel, Constance, and Jane Doe put on shepherd's hats.

NOEL. *(As Didi, French accent.)* There is no room at this inn, for it is Christmas… Shall we hang ourselves?

CONSTANCE. *(As Gogo, French accent.)* I hear it gives you an erection.

NOEL. *(As Didi, French accent.)* Then we must hang ourselves… *immediately.*

The lights shift starkly and unsettling wind blows as Noel glares at the audience intensely and smokes an imaginary cigarette. A long, uncomfortable silence.

CONSTANCE. *(Finally…as Mary…desperately uncomfortable, imagining her parents watching in the audience.)* Or…we could just go to the manger, Joseph.

[SFX #9.3: Noel's bumper pt. 2]

KARNAK. Aspiring iconoclast, enfant terrible… Noel Gruber, the most romantic boy in town.

Music out.

NOEL. I've seen the movie *The Blue Angel* about a billion and one times… If there is something better on this earth than Marlene Dietrich playing Lola Lola (the heartless boozehound harlot) I don't even want to hear about it… I tried to go as her every year for Halloween—I always chickened out… And I'd go as something like C-3PO…but in my heart, I was Lola Lola, dressed up as C-3PO…that was always my Halloween costume's subtext. Mom tells me I've got to try to blend in, so I tried really hard to dial it back… I had to…we live in a town where every year on July 11th when 7-Eleven gives out free Slurpees it's like seriously, the major cultural event of the year… I'm not even making a joke right now. It's like, a Slurpee Woodstock.

I was born in the wrong town, the wrong country, the wrong era! I wanted to feel, goddamnit. I wanted bad love. I wanted a man that would drive me to drink. I craved dissipation. I wanted to wake up in an alleyway in my own vomit, missing teeth. I wanted to drink myself to death on the cup of life…

"Anyone who hasn't experienced the ecstasy of betrayal knows nothing about ecstasy at all." Jean Genet. I was a sexual provocateur and a novelist who never wrote a novel…or had sex…

A slide comes up of Noel in a Taco Bell uniform.

NOEL. *(Slightly horrified.)* What's that?

KARNAK. I was hoping you could tell me.

NOEL. No! *(Muttering.)* I worked at the Taco Bell, in the food court of the Mega Mall just outside Uranium City. *(Defeated.)* I had to work somewhere, we had no money. I was saving up to move to France.

KARNAK. They named a meal after your passing, "The Noel Gruber Hungry Hombre Meal." They catered your funeral for free. They even played Christina Aguilera's "Beautiful" on the bagpipes.

NOEL. I only said I liked that song once. Ironically… *(Defeated.)* A joke was my final song. All those wasted hours in that horrible mall dreaming of—

KARNAK. I feel this is a perfect occasion for a song about affordable Mexican cuisine. Cue the mariachi band!

NOEL. I don't want to sing a song about that!

OCEAN. Oh! Oh! If he doesn't want to sing, I will! I will!

NOEL. Goddamnit! Can you keep it in your pants for two seconds, you horrible succubus.

Pause.

Fine.

[MUSIC #10: Noel's Lament]

During this next speech, Noel removes his clothing to reveal lingerie and puts on a wig. He transforms into a Louise Brooks femme fatale, wearing fishnet stockings and high heels.

In my life I was Noel Gruber who worked at Taco Bell in Uranium City, Saskatchewan, but…in my dreams…I played a different role. I was Monique Gibeau in postwar France…

A HOOKER WITH A HEART…OF BLACK CHARCOAL!

Accordion riff.

I WRITE POEMS TO BURN BY FIRELIGHT
DRINK CHAMPAGNE AND GUZZLE GIN
GOOD GIRLS CALL ME THE TOWN BICYCLE
DON'T KNOCK IT 'TIL YOU'VE TRIED MY LIFE OF SIN

Accordion riff.

OH, CLAUDE, MY PIMP, KNOWS NEVER MESS WITH ME
LAST PRICK DID THAT FADED QUICK TO BLACK
"I HAVE NO IDEA WHERE TO FIND HIM OFFICERS"
BUT IF YOU DO, PLEASE MENTION THAT
I'D LIKE TO HAVE RETURNED THE PRETTY KNIFE
THAT I STUCK TEN! TIMES IN! HIS! BACK

Pause. Then accordion riff.

FOR I SING SONGS UNTIL THE BREAK OF DAWN
I EMBRACE A NEW MAN EVERY NIGHT
MY LIFE'S ONE NEVER-ENDING CARNIVAL

KIDS.

A WHIRL OF BOOZY FLOOZY FLASHING LIGHT

NOEL.

I WANT TO BE THAT FUCKED-UP GIRL

Accordion riff into a pantomime dance between Noel (as Monique) and Mischa (as her suitor). It feels like an old black-and-white silent film. They meet on the street. Mischa lights Noel's cigarette. Mischa gives Noel a rose. Noel takes the rose, smells it, and pricks his finger on the thorn. Mischa suggestively kisses the finger. Noel slaps him in the face. This turns Mischa and Noel on; they tango and kiss.

Another accordion riff.

NOEL.	**GIRLS.**
HE SAID, I THINK I AM IN LOVE WITH YOU	OO
I'VE HEARD THAT LIE A MILLION TIMES BEFORE	OO
OH, TONIGHT I GIVE IN TO THE FANTASY	OO
TAKE LOVE WHEN YOU CAN	
WHEN YOU'RE A WHORE	

Accordion riff.

FOR I SING SONGS UNTIL THE BREAK OF DAWN
I COMMIT A NEW CRIME EVERY NIGHT
MY LIFE'S ONE NEVER-ENDING CARNIVAL

KIDS.

A WHIRL OF BOOZY FLOOZY FLASHING LIGHT

NOEL.

I WANT TO BE THAT FUCKED-UP GIRL

There is an extended piano riff, during which Noel further descends into pathetic, melancholy rubato.

NOEL.	**GIRLS.**
SO NOW I SELL MY LOVE FOR OPIUM	OO
IN SOME RAT-INFESTED SLATTERN DIVE	OO
AT NIGHT I BURN MYSELF WITH CIGARETTES	OO
JUST TO SOMEHOW PROVE I'M STILL ALIVE	

	KIDS (EXCEPT NOEL).
EIGHT MONTHS LATER	
I CATCH TYPHOID FLU	AH
KICKED OUT, I SEE THE UGLY	
LIGHT OF DAY	AH
DYING IN AN ALLEY, A PRIEST	
KNEELS DOWN TO ME	AH

RICKY. *(As priest, French accent.)* My child, do you have any final words to the Lord you'd like to say?

NOEL. *(As Monique.)* Oui! Tell him that I choose to burn out rather than fade away…

Accordion riff into a slow, gypsy-style buildup, eventually culminating in a total frenzy. The staging should accent the downbeat, indicated in the underlined words.

FOR I SING <u>SONGS</u> UNTIL THE <u>BREAK</u> OF DAWN
<u>I</u> EMBRACE A NEW MAN EVERY <u>NIGHT</u>
MY LIFE'S ONE <u>NE</u>VER-ENDING <u>CAR</u>NIVAL
A <u>WHIRL</u> OF BOOZY FLOOZY FLASHING <u>LIGHT</u>

FOR I SING <u>SONGS</u> UNTIL THE <u>BREAK</u> OF DAWN
<u>I</u> EMBRACE A NEW MAN EVERY <u>NIGHT</u>
MY LIFE'S ONE <u>NE</u>VER-ENDING <u>CAR</u>NIVAL

KIDS.

A WHIRL OF BOOZY FLOOZY FLASHING LIGHT

NOEL.

I WANT TO...
BE THAT FUCKED-UP GIRL!

Total frenzy with tambourines, clapping on the downbeats, shouting on upbeats, with Noel riffing on top.

TO BE THAT FUCKED-UP GIRL

GIRLS.	**GUYS.**	**NOEL.**
BROKEN HEART, A FLASK OF	HEY HEY	GIRL
GIN,	HEY HEY	
TATTOOED WITH A SAFETY	HEY HEY	
PIN!	HEY HEY	
TEETH ALL STAINED WITH	HEY HEY	
NICOTINE,	HEY HEY	
RUNNING NYLON, SHATTERED	HEY HEY	
DREAMS!	HEY HEY	
SUPER CRUSTY, HOLY TERROR	HEY HEY	GIRL
WILD EYES AND BAD MASCARA!	HEY HEY	
BROKEN HEART, A FLASK OF	HEY HEY	
GIN,	HEY HEY	GIRL
TATTOOED WITH A SAFETY	HEY HEY	
PIN!	HEY HEY	
	HEY HEY	
	HEY HEY	
TEETH ALL STAINED WITH	HEY HEY	GIRL
NICOTINE,	HEY HEY	
RUNNING NYLON, SHATTERED	HEY HEY	
DREAMS!	HEY HEY	
SUPER CRUSTY HOLY TERROR,	HEY HEY	GIRL
WILD EYES AND BAD MASCARA!	HEY HEY	
	HEY HEY	
	HEY HEY	

NOEL.	**KIDS (EXCEPT NOEL).**
IF I COULD HAVE JUST ONE DREAM	AHH

KIDS (EXCEPT NOEL).

IF HE COULD HAVE JUST ONE DREAM

NOEL.

I'D BE THAT

KIDS.
FUCKED-UP GIRL!

MISCHA.
HEY!

As the applause fades, Noel stares at Mischa, wondering what his response will be...will he say something horrible?

That... Was... *(Suddenly super enthusiastic.)* Dope! Yo! *(To Ricky.)* Ricky! You play squeeze keys mad wicked awesome.

RICKY. Heightened abilities. I can play the accordion now.

He plays a skilled accordion solo.

Level up!

OCEAN. I champion Noel's journey of sexual discovery...but he dropped the f-bomb, in the actual chorus?!

[MUSIC #11: Spooky Jane Fornication]

Tight special on Jane.

JANE.
FORNICATION UNDER CONSENT OF THE KING!

Jane, standing on a crate, rests her hand on Constance's shoulder. A chill goes through Constance's body.

CONSTANCE. ...Why?

Constance politely slinks away from Jane's hand.

(Toward Ocean.) Well, I liked the part where the two boys kissed.

MISCHA. What? In my country, it is natural for two men to show affection by kissing.

Beat.

Not always in heels...

OCEAN. There's a difference between affection and smut.

NOEL. Not in my bible, baby. Bonsoir!

[MUSIC #11A: Bonsoir!]

Curtain shuts down on Noel.

OCEAN. So, is everybody's song going to have profanity in the chorus?

MISCHA. Mine will *only* have profanity in the chorus.

CONSTANCE. *(Belly laughs, then stops cold when Ocean looks at her.)* Noooooo.

OCEAN. *(To Mischa.)* Why don't YOU go text your imaginary girlfriend?

MISCHA. I tell you before, there is no Wi-Fi, Little Orphan A-hole.

OCEAN. Noel didn't even talk about anything real. It was just a song about him wanting to be a sex worker in the old-fashioned days… What is even the moral in his song anyway? What does it teach you? What's the lesson?…

KARNAK. Not every story has a lesson, Ocean.

OCEAN. *(Like her entire worldview is being crushed.)* Nooooooo. *(Adamant, slightly hysterical.)* Every story has a lesson…

[MUSIC #12: Every Story's Got a Lesson]

Every story!

The kids, except Ocean and Noel, whistle as Ocean sings.

EVERY STORY'S GOT A LESSON
A SIMPLE MORAL TO BE TOLD
ALTHOUGH A TALE MAY
TWIST AND TURN

KIDS (EXCEPT OCEAN and NOEL).

THERE'S ALWAYS SOMETHING YOU CAN LEARN

OCEAN.

A NUGGET OF WISDOM, SOLID GOLD!

KIDS (EXCEPT OCEAN and NOEL).

SOLID GOLD!

OCEAN. Constance, improv scenario lesson number seventy-six!

CONSTANCE. Right now?!

OCEAN. Right now! Scenario seventy-six. "The Cinderella kid!"

Constance and Ocean spin around. Harp gliss as they do. Ocean magically produces a sparkly wand.

AND SCENE!

À la Glinda the Good Witch in an after-school special.

Behold! I am your fairy godmother. What's wrong?

CONSTANCE. I dunno. I just feel depressed and unmotivated lately. *(As if she's reading from the counselor's pamphlet.)* Like, I might do and/or deal recreational drugs.

OCEAN. Don't do and/or deal recreational drugs! You want to know my secret to a purpose-driven life?

CONSTANCE. *(Flatly.)* Oh boy do I.

OCEAN. Make a "to-do" list every day. And make sure you do everything on that list.

CONSTANCE. *(Mimes writing in air.)* Check!

OCEAN. You see, you're succeeding already!

CONSTANCE and OCEAN. *(Scripted laughter together.)* Ha! Ha! Ha!

OCEAN. Life's easy peasy lemon squeezy! When you…

CONSTANCE and OCEAN. "Unlock the Power of the Positive!"

Ocean does a wand drop, in the style of a mic drop.

CONSTANCE. *(Air writing, impishly.)* To do. Help the biker up the road make crystal meth, so you can do and/or deal recreational drugs!

OCEAN. STOP! STOP! *(Seething but trying to conceal it.)* What the heck was that?! That is certainly not what I scripted in this scenario!

CONSTANCE. *(Trying to hold laughter.)* I always thought that would be a funnier ending…like your motivational motivator accidentally motivated my character to…like actually do drugs… *(Dwindling into nervous laughter.)* Your character is all like "Be motivated, you!" and my character is all like "If you says so, motivational person." And like I'll go out and do all the drugs in like…the…entire…

Ocean's face is complete stone as Constance fades…

You're mad? Sorry, look, I'm still distracted. I'm still thinking about the time those two boys kissed.

MISCHA. *(Morally outraged.)* What?! Just 'cause I am rock hard, real man doesn't mean I have not seen an entire season of *RuPaul's Drag Racer*. Don't even try to put Mischa Bachinski in a box. Because I'll always break out of that shit, hunties! Enough! Let's get this party started! Make money! Make rain!

He throws pennies and crap out of his pockets.

[MUSIC #12A: Mischa's Bumper]

KARNAK. Mischa Bachinski, born August 18th, Leo: sign of aggression.

[SFX #12A.1: Mischa's photobomb]

He pulls the Karnak lever…photomontage of him as a baby to his current age.

Favorite ride: the beer garden.

Mischa mimes drinking a beer. Constance enters as his mother.

Mischa was conceived in a little town outside Odessa in Ukraine by a factory worker named Tamara. His mother, after being part of the clean-up crew in Chernobyl, was dying of prolonged exposure to uranium.

She hugs him and he waves goodbye.

Wanting her son to be safe, she decided to put him up for adoption—forging his birth certificate, she claimed he was two years old and was recently potty-trained.

Ocean and Noel play Misha's straitlaced adoptive parents; they act out the following narration.

When Mischa came to Canada, his adoptive parents were surprised to see their toddler had five o'clock shadow and a slight trace of alcohol on his breath. They put him in the basement, and his adoptive mother would prepare food and leave it for him on the top of the stairs. On the rare occasion he would run into his new parents—the mother would weep, and the father would shoo him away like a horsefly.

Mischa magically produces a handheld wireless microphone.

So began an inexhaustible rage. He turned to the last bastion of pure strength and masculinity in society: self-aggrandizing, commercialized hip-hop. This is how Mischa became the angriest boy in town.

Music out.

MISCHA. *(Into wireless mic.)* Yo! I want to talk about feeling. Ukrainian men have two emotion: Rage! And Passion. People always be hating on me and my mad skillz, 'cause I am best rapper in all of northeastern Saskatchewan. Grab yo dicks if you in the three-o-six! Brah! You might know me as "Bad Egg" on the YouTube. I'm well-known there.

That's where I met my shorty, Talia. She's from Kiev, from my country, and she gave me mostly positive feedback on my YouTube comment wall...and then we became mad passionate all-night lovers on Facebook, Twitter...we made love with each other in my native language on all of the social media networks. She is now my fiancée...we were engaged... I was saving up to move back to Ukraine and we were going to... *(Gets emotional.)* Too much passion...now Rage!

I have no respect for this country! Fact: You want to know what Canada is leading supplier of, to whole world? Two things: mustard seeds...and uranium. That's great for hot dogs, yes...but not so good for Ukraine. So thank you for killing my mother. And for indirectly killing me. I feel the rage, and when I rage, I rap about money...in auto-tune. *(Accusingly at anyone who laughs.)* Auto-tune will never die. Hit the beat.

[MUSIC #13: This Song Is Awesome]

This song is a HEAVILY auto-tuned hip-hop number—à la T-Pain. During the number, Ricky has a robot head à la 1950s boxy vintage toy variety; he moves like a robot throughout.

MISCHA. *(Spoken.)* Yo, this is a song to tell you that what you is, is what you got! And I'm here to say that:

(Auto-tuned.) I AM THE MONEY!!
WHAT YOU IS, IS WHAT YOU GOT
AND I AM THE MONEY

CONSTANCE.
(Auto-tuned.) TAKE A LOOK BABY
HE'S THE REAL CA-CHING

MISCHA.
(Raps.) LOUNGING WITH MY HOMIES, FRIDAY NIGHT SCENE

KIDS (EXCEPT MISCHA).
HO

MISCHA.
THE PLAYSTATION'S UP ON MY SIXTY-INCH SCREEN
McNUGGETS IN THE BAG, CRISTAL'S ON TAP
NEW TOOTHBRUSH FROM TIFFANY'S
(Auto-tuned.) STILL IN THE BUBBLE RAP

TRACK LIGHTS GLOWING LIKE NUCLEAR SCIENCE IS
SPARKLING ALL OVER MY STAINLESS-STEEL APPLIANCES
I'M SHINING LIKE MIDAS, I'M THE KING OF CA-CHING
EVERYTHING I TOUCH GOES BLING BLING BLING

KIDS (EXCEPT MISCHA).
HO!

MISCHA.
(Auto-tuned/sung.) MY LIFE IS AWESOME
THIS BEAT IS AWESOME

RICKY.
(Auto-tuned.) ROBOTS ARE AWESOME

CONSTANCE.
(Auto-tuned.) TAKE A LOOK BABY
HE'S THE REAL
CA-CHING

MISCHA.
(Auto-tuned.) AND I'LL
SAY IT AGAIN
MY LIFE IS AWESOME

KIDS (EXCEPT MISCHA).

HO

MISCHA.

(Auto-tuned.) THIS HOOK IS AWESOME

RICKY.

(Auto-tuned.) ROBOTS ARE AWESOME

MISCHA.

(Raps.) NOW I'M ROLLIN' IN MY CIVIE
WITH THE PUMPED-UP BASS

KIDS (EXCEPT MISCHA).

HO

MISCHA.

BLUE LIGHTS GLOWIN', THE VIPERS ON MY FACE
WE PASSING ROUND THE CHRONIC, WE PARTY ALL NIGHT
WE START TO GET THE MUNCHIES, SO WE STOP FOR A BITE

CRUISE INTO THE LOT OF THE HARD ROCK CAFE
HERE COME THE HOTTIES, HERE COME THE VALET
THE FRONT OF THE LINE, WE DON'T NEED ID

CONSTANCE.

YOUR USUAL TABLE, SIR?

MISCHA.

(Auto-tuned.) IN THE VIP,
YO
MY LIFE IS AWESOME
THIS BEAT IS AWESOME

KIDS (EXCEPT MISCHA).

HO

RICKY.

(Auto-tuned.) ROBOTS ARE AWESOME

CONSTANCE.

(Auto-tuned.) TAKE A LOOK
BABY,
HE'S THE REAL
CA-CHING

MISCHA.

(Auto-tuned.) AND I'LL
SAY IT AGAIN
MY LIFE IS AWESOME

KIDS (EXCEPT MISCHA).

HO

MISCHA.

(Auto-tuned.) AUTO-TUNE IS AWESOME

RICKY.

(Auto-tuned.) ZERO ONE, ZERO ONE, ZERO ONE ONE

Mischa unbuttons his shirt, women produce a fan and he "Ushers-out."

MISCHA.

(Auto-tune/rap.) IT'S TIME TO START THE PARTY BUT THERE AIN'T NO PARTY HERE YET SO WE GOT TO TAKE A RIDE IN MY BRAND-NEW LEARJET FEELING HOMESICK FOR MY HOMIES IN THE UKRAINE LANDING IN KIEV BEFORE WE FINISH OFF THE CHAMPAGNE	**KIDS (EXCEPT MISCHA).** HO

ROLL TO THE CLUB WHERE THE
RICH KIDS GO
THEM EUROTRASH BITCHES ALL
CHECKING OUT MY FLOW
ALL KINDS OF HOTTIES, FROM
ALL ROUND THE WORLD
BUT I FEEL THIS PAIR OF EYES,
AND THEN I SEE THIS GIRL
SHORT-AY...

My rage has subsided. A moment.

Mischa transforms, softens.

(Whispering.) I am vulnerable now.

Mischa takes out his phone, swipes. A slide comes up of Yulia Tymoshenko.

This is Yulia Tymoshenko, the most beautiful former prime minister of Ukraine. My girlfriend styles her hair just like Yulia.

Mischa swipes. Slide of Talia appears.

My girlfriend: Natalia Muruska Bolinska.

[MUSIC #14: Talia]

We hear a horn flourish followed by a cymbal crash, after which we see a video of Talia standing in the bucolic splendor of her wedding dress. What follows is a dream ballet between Mischa and his love.

My divine Talia…when I look into your almond eyes, I do not see the boy I am, but the man I must become to possess you. I want to take all the pain from your soul, and in the passion factory of my heart, transform it into functional joy.

I want to take your hand by the Cheremosh River and with all Ukraine as witness, take you as my wife.

And we shall sing and dance and drink…and then I shall whisper in your ear…

MISCHA.	**KIDS (EXCEPT MISCHA).**
"Let rivers run wild or let them be damned…"	AH
My perfect Talia,	AH
I lay my masculinity	AH
at the altar of your maidenhood.	

Song and folkloric dance: A wedding scene with video of Talia projected on white fabric, which is used as a veil and a table, as well as onto the white skirts worn by the female characters. Lyrics are simply "Talia" and "la la."

MISCHA.	**GIRLS.**
KO-HAI-YU-OO	TALIA
	TALIA
YA-TE-BE-KO-HAI-YU-OO	TALIA
TALIA, OH MY	

MISCHA.	**BOYS.**	**GIRLS.**
TALIA	LA LA LA LA	TALIA
MY TALIA	LA LA LA LA LA	TALIA
TE-BO-HO-HAI-YU	LA LA LA LA	
	LA LA LA LA LA	TALIA
	LA LA LA LA	
OH MY LOVE	LA LA LA LA LA	AH

KIDS (EXCEPT MISCHA).

LA LA LA LA LA LA
LA LA LA LA LA LA
LA LA LA LA LA LA LA LA
LA LA LA, HEY!

LA LA LA LA LA LA
LA LA LA LA LA LA
LA LA LA LA LA LA LA LA
LA LA LA, HEY!

MISCHA.		**KIDS (EXCEPT MISCHA).**
LA LA		LA LA LA
LA LA		LA LA LA LA
LA LA		LA LA LA LA LA
		LA LA LA
		LA LA LA, HEY!
LA LA		LA LA LA
LA LA LA LA LA		LA LA LA LA LA

MISCHA.	**BOYS.**	**GIRLS.**
KO-HAI-YU-OO	TALIA	LA LA LA LA
	TALIA	LA LA LA LA LA
YA-TE-BE-KO-		LA LA LA LA
HAI-YU	TALIA	LA LA LA LA LA
OO		LA LA LA LA
	TALIA	LA LA LA LA LA
TALIA, OH MY		LA LA LA LA
TALIA	TALIA	LA LA LA LA LA
		LA LA LA LA
MY TALIA	TALIA	LA LA LA LA LA
TE-BO-KO-HAI-YU		LA LA LA LA
	TALIA	LA LA LA LA LA
		LA LA LA LA
AH OH MY LOVE	AH	LA LA LA LA LA
OH	TALIA	TALIA
	MY DARLING	AH
		LA LA LA LA
		LA LA LA
OH	TALIA	TALIA
		AH
		LA LA LA LA
		LA LA LA
OH	TALIA	TALIA
	MY DARLING	AH
		LA LA LA LA LA
OH	TALIA	TALIA
	MY DARLING	

The lights shift to become a techno/disco.

MISCHA.
I WANNA GIT WIT YOU BABY

KIDS.
HEY! HEY!
HEY! HEY!

MISCHA.
I WANNA GIT WIT YOU BABY

KIDS.
HEY! HEY!
HEY! HEY!

HEY! HEY! HEY! HEY!

Everyone leaves the stage, and Mischa appears to enter the video projection, joining hands with Talia as they run away into a field.

MISCHA.
TALIA, OH MY LOVE

KIDS (EXCEPT MISCHA).
(Offstage.) AH

The song ends, leaving Mischa staring at his phone. Long beat. The cast gathers round Mischa, who is clearly lost in sadness…not really knowing what to say. Noel touches Mischa's shoulder. Mischa hugs Noel with deep affection and sadness. Noel awkwardly hugs him at first, but Mischa's stifled cries move him. He holds him in a true embrace of friendship.

OCEAN. Look at us all, bonding…not even thinking about who we will vote for. Cut down in our youth, we all died virgins.

Spotlight on Constance.

KARNAK. Constance?

CONSTANCE. *(Terrified.)* What?

KARNAK. Just thought this seemed like a perfect segue.

CONSTANCE. For what? …I don't even know what you're talking about…

Kids stare at her; she is horrified.

KARNAK. Not ready to divulge that information just yet?

CONSTANCE. …I don't um… Ocean! Why aren't you talking right now, it's weird.

OCEAN. *What?* That's ridiculous, I don't talk *all* the time. Like I'm all about the empathy here tonight, gang…look at me, empathizing with you all right now.

She forms a wan smile; she has clearly practiced for years.

MISCHA. Yo, Ricky, you go next. Why don't you express your truth as the boy who couldn't talk…AND who now plays the accordion like the world's most celebrated accordion player… *(To himself.)* Whatever the hell that dude's name is…

RICKY. I don't think people could handle what I have to say.

CONSTANCE. Just go ahead. It's fine.

Kids rhubarb words of encouragement.

RICKY. Okay… *(Pause, gathering thoughts.)* I guess you could say I'm pretty sexy on another planet. Lo, I'm the prophet from the Zolarian Starcluster, supreme of those beings that evolved from cats. There are seven suns on the planet Zolar, so the gravitational pull makes everything harder, longer, wider… *(Whispered to Ocean.)* …wetter.

Ocean grasps her tunic, by the power of Ricky's voice.

OCEAN. WHO even are you right now?!

RICKY. I'm telling you, Monkey Love Drop…

[MUSIC #14A: Ricky's Stinger]

RICKY.	**KIDS (EXCEPT RICKY).**
I'M JUST A SWINGIN'	AH
SPACE-AGE BACHELOR MAN	AH, AH

[MUSIC #14B: Ricky's Bumper]

KARNAK. Ricky Potts, born June 5th. Gemini: the dual nature.

[SFX #14B.1: Ricky's photobomb]

*He pulls the lever… Photomontage, however his personal pictures are soon replaced with classic origin scenes from comic books: Superman lifting the car as a kid, Spidey in the lab getting bit, Bruce Wayne standing over his dead parents, the Silver Surfer, etc.**

Favorite ride: the Gravitron.

He does the motion of the Gravitron. Mischa enters as Ricky's father, the pastor, wearing a cravat, large Jim Jones sunglasses, and a midway-booth stuffed snake, preaching…

Born of a semi-renowned Pentecostal pastor, Richard at a young age toured the province with his father, spreading the good news, speaking in tongues,

* A license to produce RIDE THE CYCLONE does not include a license to publicly display any third-party copyrighted, or trademarked images or logos. Licensees must acquire rights for any copyrighted images or create their own.

and handling their saw-scaled viper snake, JoJo. *The bad news* was that after witnessing JoJo give his father a lethal bite during a rousing sermon, Richard was thoroughly traumatized and lost his power of speech.

Ricky stands center stage, transforming to the state after his father has been bitten. Noel and Constance enter as Ricky's elderly grandparents.

Moving in with his grandparents, who were collectively one hundred and eighty years old, his life consisted of feeding their nineteen cats and reading the comic books he got for his birthday. Well-meaning but dotty with age, Richard's grandparents celebrated his eighth birthday every two weeks until he was seventeen.

Patronized, pushed around, and condescended to in high school, far from growing bitter, Richard developed an elaborate playground in his synapses where he became his own best friend. Ladies and gentlemen, I give you the fantasia of Richard Potts, the most imaginative boy in town.

[MUSIC #15: Space Age Bachelor Man]

Throughout this song, Ricky shifts between his meeker self and his heroic persona.

RICKY.
(Meekly.) YOU MIGHT SEE BEFORE YOU
AN ORDINARY MAN
HA! AN EARTHLY ILLUSION
ALL A PART OF THE COSMIC PLAN!

YES, LONG AGO, THEY VISITED
THOSE OTHERS FROM OUTER SPACE!
INFORMED ME I'M THE CHOSEN ONE
TO SAVE THE ZOLARIAN RACE!

It's true. Listen…

Band kicks in. Clap, clap.

MISCHA and NOEL.
(As robot cats.) RICKY, WE ARE A
DISTANT GALAXY
A GALAXY GREATLY IN NEED
OF YOUR GROOVE, YOUR
KINK-O-MATIC
POWERS
YES WE NEED YOUR FREAK-
TASTIC SEED

RICKY.	**KIDS (EXCEPT RICKY).**
(Meekly.) THEY TOOK ME THEN	AH
TO THEIR DAUGHTERS' REALM	AH
THE LAND OF THE KITTY CAT STAR	AH, AH
I KNOW YOU'VE HEARD	AH
THE LEGENDS OF	AH

KIDS.

THE SEXY CAT WOMEN FROM ZOLAR!

Clap, clap.

GIRLS.

ME-OW-OW, ME-OW-OW

CONSTANCE.

(British accent.) MAKE LOVE TO ME

GIRLS.

(Whispered.) RICKY

RICKY.

WHAT?

GIRLS.

ME-OW-OW, ME-OW-OW

RICKY.

(Meekly.) OKAY.

OCEAN. *(Pleading.)* And there's one more thing…won't you please help save our galaxy!

RICKY. *(Big pause, noncommitally.)* …Sure?

Beat kicks in.

(Heroically.) WHAT WOULD YOU
DO IN MY PLACE?
A MERE MORTAL MAN?
THE FATE OF A GALAXY BEFORE
YOU
MILLIONS OF LIVES IN YOUR
HAND?!

RICKY.	**KIDS (EXCEPT RICKY).**
THE NAUGHTY DAUGHTERS	AH
OF THE REALM	AH
ALL HUNGRY FOR MY CHI	AH
YOU'D NEVER GUESS	AH, AH

THE ROLE I PLAY — AH
IN ZOLARIAN HISTORY! — AH

I'M JUST A SWINGIN' — AH, AH
SPACE-AGE — AH, AH
BACHELOR MAN!

Dance beat starts in…

RICKY. Let's daaance, kitties!

During the dance, Ricky and the cat women from Zolar go behind the curtain. Music is a '60s go-go style dance romp with ping-ponging meows.

GIRLS.	**RICKY.**
MEOW	
	MEOW
MEOW	
	MEOW
MEOW	
	MEOW
MEOW	
	MEOW
MEOW	
	MEOW
MEOW	
	MEOW
MEOW	
	WOOF

GIRLS and RICKY.

MEOW MEOW, MEOW MEOW MEOW

RICKY. *(Meekly.)* It gets weird now.

Clap, clap.

MISCHA and NOEL.

(As robot cats.) RICKY, YOU'VE LAIN WITH OUR DAUGHTERS
YOU'RE OUR HERO, OUR SAVING GRACE
BUT NOW THERE IS A NEW CHALLENGE
FOR ZOLARIA TO FACE

Curtain rises, revealing Ricky in an amazing space outfit à la 1970s David Bowie.

RICKY.	**KIDS (EXCEPT RICKY).**
(Heroically.) FOR THEY'RE AT WAR WITH K-9	AH

COUNT DOG-U-LOUS THAT SON OF A BITCH	AH
	THAT SON OF A BITCH
THE GENERALS ARE ALL STANDING BY	AH

KIDS.

TELL US RICKY SHOULD WE PULL THE SWITCH?

Clap, clap.

KIDS.

MEOW-OW-OW, MEOW-OW-OW

RICKY. *(Meekly.)* Oh my goodness, what have I gotten myself into?!

KIDS.

MEOW-OW-OW, MEOW-OW-OW

RICKY. *(Meekly.)* I mean, I'm a lover not a fighter…
I thought I told them…

RICKY.	**KIDS (EXCEPT RICKY).**
(Heroically.) I'M JUST A SWINGIN'	AH, AH
SPACE-AGE	AH, AH
BACHELOR MAN!	

Drum fills for '80s pop ballad set up.

RICKY. And so I told them…

I AM JUST A MAN
A SPACE-AGE MAN
THAT'S ALL I AM
BUT I WANNA HOLD YOUR HAND
ALL YOUR HANDS
WHILE WE MAKE LOVE TONIGHT

RICKY.	**KIDS (EXCEPT RICKY).**
I HAVE NO DESIRE	OO
TO RULE THE GALAXY	(OO)
OH, TO HOLD YOU CLOSE	(OO)
IT'S ENOUGH FOR ME	(OO)
MAKING LOVE IN ZERO GRAVITY	(OO)

KIDS.

OH

Ricky ad-libs riffs while kids sing.

KIDS (EXCEPT RICKY).

MAKIN' LOVE!
MAKIN' LOVE!
MAKIN' LOVE!
OH JUST LOVE ZOLAR!

MAKIN' LOVE!
MAKIN' LOVE!
MAKIN' LOVE!
OH, OH JUST LOVE ZOLAR!
MAKIN' LOVE!

RICKY.	**KIDS (EXCEPT RICKY).**
YOU'RE MY CATNIP	MAKIN' LOVE!
YOU'RE THE MOST	MAKIN' LOVE!
YOU'RE SUCH PRETTY	OH OH JUST
GRITTY KITTIES	LOVE ZOLAR!
	MAKIN' LOVE!
I WANNA BE	MAKIN' LOVE!
YOUR SCRA-HATCHIN'	
POST, LET ME BE, LET ME BE	MAKIN' LOVE!
LET ME BE	JUST LOVE

RICKY. *(Meekly.)* And they listened. And they heard my message. For I was singing notes that only cats or cat people could hear. A G-sharp, 5 octaves above middle C.

Music stops, pause; cats react. One cat sprays itself with a bottle of hair spray.

Incredible. Peace was restored. I guess that's what happens

RICKY.	**KIDS (EXCEPT RICKY).**
(Heroic switch.) WHEN YOU'RE A SWINGIN'	AH
SPACE-AGE	AH
BACHELOR MAN!	
SO I CAME BACK TO EARTH	AH
TO SHOW YOU THE WAY	AH
TO LEAD YOU PRETTY PEOPLE	AH
TO A BRIGHTER DAY-AY-AY	AH
WE CAN SAVE THE WHOLE GALAXY	AH
WITH LOVE FROM THE HEART!	AH
AND SEXY CAT LADIES	AH
IS WHERE WE GOTTA START!	AH

YES, I CAME BACK TO THIS ROCK — AH
WITH MY LOVE AND MY SEED. — AH
LADIES, YOU GOT WHAT I WANT — AH
AND YOU KNOW I'VE GOT WHAT YOU NEED! — AH

'CAUSE I'M A SWINGIN'
SPACE-AGE
B-B-B-B-BACHELOR MAN!

KIDS (EXCEPT RICKY).
BACHELOR! MAN! MEOW!

MISCHA. Dude, you are so awesome in the afterlife!

RICKY. *(Meekly.)* I'm the same person I always was, it's just no one ever listened to me on earth.

MISCHA. We'll listen to you now, Space Jesus.

RICKY. I guess all I have to say is this: If sacred places are spared the ravages of war…then make all places sacred. And if the holy people are to be kept harmless from war…then make all people holy.

NOEL. …Did you write that?

RICKY. No, it was the Silver Surfer.

CONSTANCE. I am so happy right now! I can never come down!

JANE. My turn.

CONSTANCE. Aww man.

[MUSIC #15A: Jane Doe's Bumper]

KARNAK. Jane Doe, the one unidentified body of the Cyclone roller coaster disaster.

[SFX #15A.1: Jane's photobomb]

She goes to pull the lever; a sound effect happens, but no photos appear.

Everyone knew everyone in Uranium, but no one could recall this member of the choir. There were rumors of a girl who joined at the last minute but as the choir conductor Father Markus died of a heart attack seven hours after the accident, there was no one left to verify. Some believe that perhaps she was never in the choir at all. I never read her fortune; I sadly cannot tell you. All one knows for certain is that a body was found in a Saint Cassian uniform, without a head. So, a mystery.

[MUSIC #16: The Ballad of Jane Doe]

In this number, the children are dressed in funeral garb, with bowler hats and trench coats to conceal them and their faces…almost like faceless Magritte figures.

JANE.
SOME MIGHT SAY WE'RE RELEASED
PUSHING DAISIES, DECEASED
BUT WE ALL KNOW THE WORMS
MUST BE FED

THERE'S JUST ONE LINGERING
FEAR
OH MY SOUL, IS IT HERE?
OR IS IT ROTTING SOMEWHERE
WITH MY HEAD?

JANE.
OH MY SOUL
OH MY SOUL
OH MY SOUL
OH MY SOUL

KIDS (EXCEPT JANE).
BUP BUP BAH
BUP BUP BAH
BUP BUP BAH
AH

KIDS.
OO
AH

Curtain is slowly opened to reveal a funeral picture. The children with umbrellas create a silhouette of a family at a grave on a rainy day. Their backs are to the audience.

JANE.
OH NO SOUL, AND NO NAME
AND NO STORY, WHAT A SHAME
CRUEL EXISTENCE WAS ONLY A SHAM

OH SAINT PETER, LET ME IN!
YOU MUST KNOW WHERE I'VE BEEN
WON'T YOU TELL ME AT LAST WHO I AM?

JANE.
WHO I AM
WHO I AM
WHO I AM
WHO I AM

KIDS (EXCEPT JANE).
BUP BUP BAH
BUP BUP BAH
BUP BUP BAH
AH

KIDS.

OO
AH

The children slowly move from their funeral vignette with a broken mechanical doll quality to several podiums, mechanically forming grief poses.

JANE.

AND FROM THE GROUND, BENEATH MY FEET
I HEAR THE ANGUISH OF THE STREET

KIDS (EXCEPT JANE).

A CHOIR NEVER COMPLETE

JANE.

AND LIKE AN OLD FORGOTTEN TUNE,
A SONG THAT NO ONE KNOWS!
FORGOT HOW IT GOES!
JUST JOHN AND ME FOREVER
ETERNALLY, JANE DOE!

As the beat kicks in, this next sequence is staged to feel like all the rides in the warehouse are coming to life, creating the image of a fairground at night. All the children's umbrellas light up with LEDs: a large patio umbrella lights up, making it look like a carousel; another umbrella looks like a Ferris wheel; another closed umbrella lights up to resemble the Salt and Pepper Shaker. The CYCLONE sign, the proscenium, and any practical that can light up in the context of design, lights up now.

<table>
<tr><td>JANE.</td><td></td></tr>
<tr><td>AND I'M ASKING</td><td>KIDS (EXCEPT JANE).</td></tr>
<tr><td>WHY LORD?</td><td>WHY LORD?</td></tr>
<tr><td>IF THIS IS HOW I DIE, LORD</td><td>DIE, LORD</td></tr>
<tr><td>WHY BE LEFT WITH NO FAMILY</td><td></td></tr>
<tr><td>AND NO FRIENDS</td><td>OO</td></tr>
<tr><td>I'VE GOT NO CELEBRATION</td><td>'BRATION</td></tr>
<tr><td>JUST THIS CONSOLATION</td><td>'LATION</td></tr>
</table>

TIME EATS ALL HIS CHILDREN IN THE END

Arpeggio riffing.

AH

A MELODY FLOATS THROUGH THE AIR
WHEN SILENCE FALLS, DOES NO ONE CARE?

KIDS (EXCEPT JANE).

DOES ANYONE CARE?

JANE.

ANOTHER SAD FORGOTTEN TUNE
ANOTHER SONG THAT NO ONE KNOWS!
SO THAT'S HOW IT GOES!
JUST JOHN AND ME
FOREVER ETERNALLY JANE DOE

KIDS (EXCEPT JANE).

AND SHE'S ASKING

WHY LORD?

THIS IS NO WAY TO DIE, LORD

JANE.

WHY, OH WHY,
WHY, OH
OH WHY?

JANE.

NO ONE TO SING, NO ONE TO SIGH
NOW THAT ALL IS SAID AND DONE
ISN'T THERE ANYONE TO TELL ME WHO I AM?

KIDS (EXCEPT JANE).

OO
NO SINGIN' SONGS OF CELEBRATION
JUST THIS SORRY SPECULATION

JANE.

AH
(AH)

JANE.

LIKE JOHN I'LL BE, ETERNALLY
A FORGOTTEN NAME, SOME LOST REFRAIN
JUST JANE
JANE
DOE!

KIDS (EXCEPT JANE).

A MELODY FLOATS THROUGH THE AIR
WHEN SILENCE FALLS, DOES NO ONE CARE?
JANE! DOE!

[MUSIC #16A: The Ballad of Jane Doe Playoff]

Constance lights a cupcake with a birthday candle in the darkness. Silence. Ocean walks up and puts a birthday hat on Jane. They sing "Happy Birthday" a cappella.

KIDS (EXCEPT JANE).
(Gently, delicately, like singing to a baby in a crib.) HAPPY BIRTHDAY TO YOU
HAPPY BIRTHDAY TO YOU
HAPPY BIRTHDAY DEAR…

CONSTANCE. *(Searching for the name.)* …Hmmm mmm…

OCEAN. *(Trying to save it.)* Ah…that song's so overplayed. We'll come up with something better.

[MUSIC #17: The New Birthday Song]

Ricky at the glockenspiel/harmonium/whatever. Ocean starts singing, teaching all "The New Birthday Song." They slowly join in over the first round until they are full swing.

This should feel like it is being composed on the spot, Ocean struggling for the words as she makes them up.

OCEAN.
ONE TWO THREE
ONE TWO THREE
ONE TWO THREE…

(Searchingly.) FOUR?

THIS IS THE NEW SONG WE SING FOR BIRTHDAYS!

KIDS (EXCEPT JANE).
BOUNCY AND MERRY AND NOT QUITE AS SCARY
THE NEW BIRTHDAY SONG

They dance around Jane. The song ends and Constance offers Jane the cupcake. Music continues.

CONSTANCE. It's a cupcake. For you.

Jane stares at her, then takes the cupcake and walks away. Cross-fade to Ricky and Jane playing with a glockenspiel.

JANE. How do we know it's my birthday?

RICKY. …How do we know it's *not* your birthday?

JANE. People have names on pretend birthdays, too.

RICKY. You could call yourself Savannah…

JANE. What's a Savannah?

RICKY. Savannah is a special name I was saving up, but you can have it. 'Cause everything I've been saving has to go. It's a fire sale in my brain, and everything must go, by *(Echo in his voice.)* m-m-m-midnight.

JANE. I like Savannah.

RICKY. You can have her.

JANE. Can Savannah have the greenest eyes?

RICKY. Yes.

JANE. ...Savannah...with the greenest eyes.

Cross-fade to Mischa and Noel. Mischa takes a swig from a vodka bottle then offers it to Noel.

MISCHA. Drink?

NOEL. Where'd you get that?

MISCHA. *(Shrugs.)* It's birthday.

Noel chugs vodka.

NOEL. *(Takes a deep swig.)* I've never been drunk before... *(Takes another swig.)* ...or kissed a man. Thank you.

MISCHA. Budmo! *(Translating.)* May we live forever...

Mischa and Noel smile at each other bittersweetly.

And your life was tragic. Cut down before the poems could ever come out of you. You are tragic.

NOEL. You think so?

MISCHA. *(Sincerely.)* You make me weep just looking at you. So, so tragic...

NOEL. That is the nicest thing anyone has ever said to me.

Cross-fade to...

CONSTANCE. ...That was nice of you...throwing that party for that girl like that.

OCEAN. It's what I do. Strange, in our predicament she's somehow the saddest.

CONSTANCE. I totally agree.

OCEAN. *(Sharply turns to Constance.)* You're not thinking of voting for her, are you?

CONSTANCE. No, I'm voting for you! Naturally! Of course! Ocean... um...do you think you'd ever kind of like...vote for me?

OCEAN. Of course I would, you're my best friend...but it's by a unanimous vote...so I kind of have to...

CONSTANCE. *(Flatly.)* Vote for yourself.

OCEAN. *(Grabs Constance's hand.)* You know I envy you?

CONSTANCE. No you don't, Ocean.

OCEAN. No I do… I mean I got straight As since I was in grade one. I was working toward something. I was building a life. You, you were satisfied doing nothing, making cupcakes…eating them. You are what the Taoists call an "uncarved block."

CONSTANCE. *(Incredulous but restrained.)* I'm a block?

OCEAN. Just learn to take a compliment.

CONSTANCE. *(Seething.)* Thanks…

OCEAN. I thought my life had meaning, turns out it didn't. Oh well, joke's on me… *(Sobbing.)* My death has really affected me.

CONSTANCE. *(Gritting.)* Yeah, me too.

OCEAN. *(Sobbing uncontrollably.)* Naturally, my death has affected you—can't you just listen for once without making it about yourself?

Constance punches Ocean in the boob. Music stops.

OWCH! You just punched me! …In the frickin' boob!

CONSTANCE. *(Not sorry.)* Sorry.

[MUSIC #17A: Constance's Bumper]

KARNAK. Constance Blackwood, born November 14th. Scorpio: the secret nature.

[SFX #17A.2: Constance's photobomb]

She pulls the lever…photomontage.

Favorite ride: the Cyclone. The only honor Constance Blackwood was to receive in her short lifetime was "nicest girl in homeroom." Three years in a row. An award she secretly threw in the dumpster behind her local Kentucky Fried Chicken on her way home. When the children of Saint Cassian signed Constance's yearbook, they wrote things like…

RICKY. …Wow, you seemed so nice…

KARNAK. …Or…

NOEL. …I never really met you—you seemed friendly.

KARNAK. Those pages in Constance's yearbook were carefully removed with an X-ACTO knife. And burned. Constance Blackwood, the nicest girl in town.

CONSTANCE. *(Bluntly, frankly.)* So I lost my virginity to a carnie in a porta-potty before I died. Like three hours before. It was kind of porno. He was like ancient, like thirty-two. And he had this tattoo on his forearm…it was of two skeletons having sex, and it said "Born to Bone" on the bottom of it.

Light up on Mischa wearing the Iron Maiden shirt.

MISCHA. *(As a carnie.)* Isn't my tattoo the stupidest thing you've ever seen?

Constance laughs.

CONSTANCE. I fake laughed when he said that because you should always laugh at guys' jokes, or they'll think you're a cow. My mom and dad own the Blackwood Café in town. It's been in our family since, like forever. The Blackwoods have been in Uranium since they opened the mines…my family had pride when it came to that. 'Til I went to high school and having pride about our town was only like the lamest thing you could ever think to believe. After a while, I started feeling kind of crummy about stuff, like ashamed. At the café, I would catch myself looking at my mom thinking, "What a loser, a stupid dead-end loser, in a stupid dead-end town." My parents were good people and all I could do was think horrible things about them. I really wish I never thought those things… But I got so angry that I was born in the only family in Uranium that raised their kid to think it was okay to do your working, living, and dying there. And it just got all kinds of poison after that.

Anyway, my virginity…I just wanted to get it out of the way. I just wanted to do it, so I didn't have to think about doing it anymore. No, actually… I just wanted to lose it in the most horrible possible way. "Constance the lifer, lost it to a carnie, in a crap box, in a crappy town! Why, of course she did…"

And then I rode the Cyclone with the other kids in the choir…and that's when the accident happened.

[MUSIC #17B: Guitar Sugarcloud Underscore]

With growing intensity and speed throughout, a volcano of memories.

We were at the top of the loop when the roller coaster made this kind of screaming metal sound. Sparks were shooting all over the place. And then the screaming and the sparks just stopped…and there was like this weightlessness… My heart jumped like a gazillion beats a second, but I didn't scream like the other kids… No, I was just soaking it all in, 'cause on a certain level it was so rad…sailing through the air upside down, you could see all the other rides. And it was like something unlocked in me; my heart just welled up with all this love for everything.

Images and all this feeling flooded into me. Like climbing back into my bed in the morning and feeling the heat left over from my body, hanging upside down from the monkey bars until my head starts to tingle, smelling jiffy markers, listening to music and dancing around my room before going out to a party and pretending I'm going to have the perfect time, licking maple syrup off French toast Sunday morning, finishing an essay, undoing a knot, pizza night, Halloween, watching my baby brother dance naked to ABBA, being in the choir during the height of the Hallelujah chorus and feeling all the voices rattle my bones. And I started laughing like a crazy person, giddy with endorphins, all dancing leprechauns and rainbows and unicorns, streams of chocolate, whirling rides, flashing lights.

There's no shame in loving my small town. The only good things that happened to me happened in Uranium. It took a horrible accident for me to realize how goddamn wonderful everything is.

[MUSIC #18: Jawbreaker/Sugarcloud]

CONSTANCE.

I USED TO THINK THAT LIFE WAS JUST A JAWBREAKER
YEAH, YOU SUCK, AND YOU SUCK
AND YOU SUCK, AND YOU SUCK
AND YOU SUCK SOME MORE
YEAH, YOU SUCK SOME MORE

CONSTANCE.	**KIDS (EXCEPT CONSTANCE).**
AT FIRST IT SEEMS SO SWEET	OO
AND THE COLORS COME AND GO	
LIKE THE SEASONS COME AND GO	OO
THE SLUSH AND RAIN AND SNOW	
'TIL YOU CAN'T TASTE NO MORE	OO
SO YOU SUCK SOME MORE	SO YOU SUCK SOME MORE
I USED TO THINK THAT LIFE	AAH
WAS JUST A HEARTBREAKER	
THAT JUST BREAKS, AND IT BREAKS	AAH
AND IT BREAKS, AND IT BREAKS	
'TIL IT CAN'T BREAK NO MORE	AAH
'TIL	

KIDS.

YOU CAN'T TAKE NO MORE

AH
OO
AH
OO

This next part of the number should feel like a rock concert. Constance should have a microphone, and Mischa and Noel should ideally play trombones. Lighting-wise, this is the brightest number in the show… Imagine the pinkness of the sky gradually giving way to a glorious sunrise.

CONSTANCE.

I SEE THE WORLD
WITH ALL ITS BACKWARDS UPSIDE DOWNS
THERE'S NOTHIN' WRONG
WITH BEIN' THE NICEST GIRL IN TOWN

OH EVERYTHING'S CLEAR
NOW THAT I'M HERE
ON MY SUGAR CLOUD

CONSTANCE.

OH MY SOUL IT SINGS A SONG
SO SWEET AND PURE
I'VE FELT IT ALL ALONG
BUT NOW I'M SURE
OH EVERYTHING'S LOVE
LOOKIN' DOWN FROM ABOVE
ON MY SUGAR CLOUD

LET ME
TAKE YOU AWAY
TO A SKY OF COTTON CANDY
FLYING LIKE A KITE ON A
STRING!

UP, UP, UP AND ABOVE
ALL THAT SUGAR-COATED
DANDY
I WOULDN'T CHANGE
MY LIFE FOR A THING!
IT MAKES ME WANT TO SING!

I SEE THE GOLD, I SEE THE PINK
I SEE THE BLUE,
THE SUN GOES UP
THE SUN GOES DOWN
OH WHAT TO DO?

KIDS (EXCEPT CONSTANCE).

AH OO SHA LA LA
AH OO
AH OO SHA LA LA
AH OO
AH OO SHA LA LA
AH OO
AH OO SHA LA LA
OO LA LA LA LA
LA LA LA LA
AHH

FLYING LIKE A KITE
ON A STRING!

AH
AH AH

I WOULDN'T CHANGE
MY LIFE FOR A THING!

AH OOH SHA LA LA
AH OOH SHA LA LA
AH OOH
SHA LA LA
AH OOH SHA LA LA

OH EVERYTHING'S CLEAR,
NOW THAT I'M HERE
ON MY SUGAR CLOUD

AH OOH SHA LA LA
AH OOH SHA LA LA
AH OOH SHA LA LA
OO LA LA LA LA LA!

Instrumental section. Constance plays a badass recorder solo.

KIDS (EXCEPT CONSTANCE).
I USED TO THINK THAT LIFE
WAS JUST A JAWBREAKER
YOU SUCK, AND YOU SUCK
THEN YOU SUCK SOME MORE!
I USED TO THINK THAT LIFE
WAS JUST A HEARTBREAKER

CONSTANCE.
(Ad-libbing.) JAWBREAKER!

KIDS.
IT BREAKS AND IT TAKES 'TIL
YOU CAN'T TAKE NO MORE!

CONSTANCE.
AND NOW I'M FLOATING HIGH
ON A CLOUD
AND I COULD PUKE A RAINBOW!

Jane and Ocean release a confetti cannon over the audience, ideally on beat, following the final "LA"! The lights are at their brightest; the sun has risen.

KIDS (EXCEPT CONSTANCE and MISCHA).
(Rainbow/waterfall-like.) AH

KIDS (EXCEPT CONSTANCE).
LA LA LA LA LA

CONSTANCE.
I SEE THE WORLD
WITH ALL ITS BACK-
WARDS UPSIDE
DOWNS
THERE'S NOTHIN'
WRONG
WITH BEIN' THE
NICEST GIRL IN
TOWN

GIRLS.
OH, SHE SEES
THE WORLD
WITH ALL OF
ITS DARK
AND ITS
LIGHT

GUYS.
OH, ALL OF THE
DARKNESS
AND ALL OF THE
BRIGHT
ALL COME TO-
GETHER
IN A BEAUTIFUL
LIGHT

CONSTANCE.
OH EVERYTHING'S CLEAR
NOW THAT I'M HERE
ON MY SUGAR CLOUD

KIDS.
EVERYTHING IS CLEAR
HERE ON MY SUGAR CLOUD

<table>
<tr><td></td><td>AH OO SHA LA LA</td></tr>
<tr><td>OH, NOW EVERYTHING
IS LOVE
LOOKIN' DOWN FROM
ABOVE</td><td>YES EVERYTHING IS LOVE</td></tr>
<tr><td>ON MY SUGAR CLOUD</td><td>HERE ON MY SUGAR CLOUD
AH OO SHA LA LA</td></tr>
<tr><td>OH NOW EVERYTHING
IS CLEAR</td><td>AH OO</td></tr>
<tr><td>NOW THAT I'M HERE
ON MY
(Ad lib.) SUGAR
CLOUD!</td><td>AH OO SHA LA LA
AH OO SHA LA LA</td></tr>
<tr><td>LOOK AT ME NOW ON MY
SUGAR CLOUD!</td><td>AH OO
SUGAR CLOUD!</td></tr>
</table>

CONSTANCE. Thanks, guys.

[MUSIC #18A: Sugarcloud Transition]

In this transition, Ocean holds the hand of Constance, as if seeing her friend for the first time. She whispers to her wordlessly, "I'm sorry." They hug.

KARNAK. Final vote.

[SFX #18A.1: Final vote trill]

Ocean Rosenberg.

A light falls on Ocean, who stares, lost, clearly moved by Constance's number. The other children are suddenly frozen in respective poses in specials—still. Frozen in statues of their characters.

OCEAN. Huh?

KARNAK. It has been decided that you shall have the final vote.

OCEAN. Over what?

KARNAK. Who lives or dies.

OCEAN. ...I thought we all had to vote on that? That's what you told us.

KARNAK. I've decided the final vote will come down to the one with the highest-grade point average. You are the winner.

OCEAN. That doesn't strike me as very fair.

KARNAK. In five minutes, all bets are off.

OCEAN. What happens in five minutes?

KARNAK. My appointment with a rat named Virgil. And then my death. After that, I'm not entirely sure.

OCEAN. Um…and if I just vote for myself, what is the moral? If I chose myself…if I choose myself, the moral of the story is that humans suck.

KARNAK. That would be a valid interpretation, yes.

OCEAN. No, no, no we're going to honor the original agreement. We will all vote on who comes back.

[MUSIC #19: Dream of Jane's Life]

The curtain slowly rises, revealing a majestic light and smoke.

What's that?

KARNAK. The Other Side. You merely walk in… It's easy, just don't look back…

Beat.

I don't mean to rush you, but Time is pressing—

OCEAN. Look if you could just kindly step off for three seconds. *(To herself.)* "The one who wants to win it the most shall redeem the loser—in order to complete the whole."

Beat.

…You knew all along I could never do it.

KARNAK. What?

OCEAN. Choose myself.

She looks around the room. She exhales.

(To everyone in the room.) It shouldn't be me.

She looks at Constance, who looks at Jane; Ocean nods.

We died young, by total accident. But to say that if one dies young, they die needlessly—that is to discount the years they had. The experiences they had… I would gladly take my seventeen years over nothing. Who do I vote for? …The girl who can't remember any of it. Her…we had a life—she didn't. That's my vote.

[MUSIC #19A: Jane Doe Video]

Ocean checks in with all the kids; they gently nod in agreement.

Motioned carried. Democracy rocks.

KARNAK. As you wish.

Jane looks confused as the kids urge her into the proscenium. She enters it; a scrim comes down, and we see her transform.

*The children move closer to the screen, which suddenly projects images at a dizzying speed, too abstract for the audience to parse. The children are transfixed.**

Her name is Penny Lamb, born April 7th. Aries: the lucky nature.

OCEAN.

IT'S NOT A GAME
MAYBE THAT'S NEWS
'CAUSE NO ONE WILL WIN HERE
AND NO ONE CAN LOSE
THERE'S NO ONE TO MEASURE
OUR FOOLISH PRIDE
AND NO ONE KEEPS SCORE
OF HOW HARD WE TRIED

OCEAN and CONSTANCE.

THIS RIDE IT HAS HEARTBREAK
THIS RIDE IT HAS PAIN

OCEAN, CONSTANCE, and NOEL.

ALL KINDS OF BLUE SKIES
NO SHORTAGE OF RAIN

KIDS (EXCEPT JANE).

YES THERE IS LAUGHTER
AND THE TELLING OF LIES
AND MAYBE IN DARKNESS
WE OPEN OUR EYES?

AND YOU GIVE AND CHOOSE
WHILE YOU LOVE AND LOSE
AND YOU FEEL THE WORLD IS SPINNING
WITH NO ENDING OR BEGINNING
YOU JUST TAKE A LOOK AROUND
TAKE A LOOK AROUND
TAKE A LOOK AROUND
AND ROUND AND ROUND AND ROUND

As this ends and the children gather to brace for their end, a countdown appears on the screen, like in an old Super 8 film... 10... 9... 8...

* See page 63 for recommended content for the Jane Doe video.

KARNAK. And now you're probably wondering what happens next…

7… 6…

That, I couldn't possibly tell you…

5… 4…

But I do know this for certain…

3…

After reading thousands of human fortunes…

2…

My final insight is…

1. Music out.

[SFX #19A.1: Karnak's death]

Suddenly, a flurry of fortunes Karnak has given over his life overlap: "You will get a promotion…" "Your love will last…" "The truth is on your side…" etc.

(Fully comprehensible.) Your lucky number is seven. You will soar to great heights. Be sure to Ride the Cyclone.

Karnak is dead, but the children remain huddled together, breathing heavily. Lights shift. Ocean breaks off from the children in contemplation. The children are baffled that they are still around…after Karnak died? Where are they? What's next? They are elated and terrified all at the same time. They gradually build up the courage to sing, unaccompanied, tentatively.

[OPTIONAL SFX #19A.2: Low B Flat buzz]

[MUSIC #20: Sailing Reprise]

CONSTANCE.
WE'RE JUST

KIDS (EXCEPT OCEAN).
SAILING THROUGH SPACE

MISCHA.
THERE'S NO

KIDS (EXCEPT OCEAN).
UP OR DOWN

NOEL.
SO

KIDS (EXCEPT OCEAN).
BEAUTIFUL AND STRANGE

RICKY.
BUT IT'S

KIDS (EXCEPT OCEAN).
MORE THAN SPINNING ROUND

YES IT'S EVERYTHING YOU LOVED
AND EVERYTHING YOU DREAMED
AND EVERYTHING YOU SHARED
AND EVERYTHING THAT SEEMED SO
OH SO TERRIFYING

[MUSIC #21: It's Just a Ride]

OCEAN.
BUT IT'S NOT A GAME, IT'S NOT A GAME

KIDS (EXCEPT JANE).
WHOA NO NO
IT'S NOT A GAME, IT'S NOT A GAME

KIDS.
(*With Jane, who sings offstage.*) IT'S JUST A RIDE!
IT'S JUST A RIDE!

WE'RE ALL JUST SAILING THROUGH SPACE
THERE'S NO UP, THERE'S NO DOWN
IT'S ALL SO BEAUTIFUL AND STRANGE
BUT SO MUCH MORE THAN SPINNING ROUND

YES IT'S EVERYTHING YOU LOVED
AND IT'S EVERYTHING YOU DREAMED
AND IT'S EVERYTHING YOU SHARED
AND IT'S EVERYTHING THAT SEEMED SO

OH SO TERRIFYING
TURN IT ROUND!

IT'S JUST A RIDE!
IT'S JUST A RIDE!

AND THE WORLD WILL KEEP ON SPINNING
WITH NO ENDING OR BEGINNING
SO JUST TAKE A LOOK AROUND

TAKE A LOOK AROUND
TAKE A LOOK AROUND

KIDS (EXCEPT JANE).
AND ROUND AND ROUND AND ROUND

JANE.
(Offstage.) I KNOW THIS DREAM OF LIFE IS NEVER-ENDING
IT GOES AROUND AND ROUND AND ROUND AGAIN

The children disappear from the stage. We see the curtain shoot up, see the eternity light, with only the sound of howling wind for a brief moment…then the curtain suddenly shoots down with the sound of the roller coaster track. The instant it hits the floor, snap blackout.

[MUSIC #22: Bows]

[MUSIC #23: Exit Music]

End of Play

RECOMMENDED CONTENT FOR THE JANE DOE VIDEO

The most effective version of the video is shot entirely from the point of view of Penny Lamb (Jane Doe's true identity). We see a flurry of images of her *from her perspective:* being born, learning to walk, going to the park, see-sawing, eating ice cream, birthday parties, putting a sweater away in a cubby, scrapping her knee, learning to write, baking, going to a school dance, watching fireworks, etc…leading to the final selfie where we see Penny's smiling face for the first time at seventeen in a Saint Cassian uniform.

www.ingramcontent.com/pod-product-compliance
Lightning Source LLC
LaVergne TN
LVHW080205180826
845678LV00023BA/1755

* 9 7 8 0 8 2 2 2 4 5 9 2 6 *